A Journey on Wings

by

Lenore T. Miles

Copyright © 2016 by Lenore T. Miles

All rights reserved. Printed in the United States.

ISBN 978-1-62806-113-0

Library of Congress Control Number 2016954812

Published by Salt Water Media
29 Broad Street, Suite 104
Berlin, MD 21811
www.saltwatermedia.com

Cover image provided courtesy by Gail Long.

Dedication:

With love, understanding, and appreciation, I dedicate this book to my family and wonderful son. Keep the faith and always believe you can make it no matter what. Trying is better than not. All things are possible. Be blessed and thankful.

Thanks

Never forget our veterans. I am one and there are others, whether past and present. We served and never let them down, because each one is very special in their way. Some still here and others gone, bless them all and their families too. One by one we salute.

Thanks for giving me support, taking your time to read my book. Hope you enjoy it. Stay open-minded. A lot of people write, but this is important to me. It took a while, but I wasn't going to stop. My goal is to truly help others that's what matters when the book goes far. I want to thank each and everyone who cares. My original poems in a book - wow! - I can say I did it with pray and praise, made it possible for this to really happen. Read on and enjoy.

In rembrance of loved ones...
The love lives on.
Never forget.

A Black Woman's Point of View

Be strong for that is the word, to say
A lady turn into a woman with many ideas and solutions
To have strength and to be alive
To keep the family as one
With love, respect, kindness and good manners
Can bring the wonder of all little children of the world together
To read and understand what the different ethnics can bring and carry
To keep peace and fulfill the hopes to pray and be thankful for all
We have what we got to maintain spiritually
And rejoice with faith and glory
To cry and be sad is really our weakness
So lift your head all black women
Be strong but stay black forever
We choose so let us choose wisely
Take a stand and help each other
Learn to be there for each other
Let's stand together as one woman to another woman with respect
Treat any woman like you would want to be treated
And we can make it

A Broken Heart

You said that you did care
With words not pleasing to the ears
I try to talk to you, didn't really listen
Open my heart and couldn't close it shut
It hurts so much I thought you would be there
But it didn't happen
How many years, when we first met
Eye to eye, we looked and looked
I guess we wouldn't have made a book
My heart is sadden and very weak
How can I mend it from too many decisions and lack of sleep
Help me fix this broken heart
Can you, will you try again to put it back together as one
Your heart

A Child's Hand

While he sits in front of me and reached his hand to be, touch and held by me. I held it tightly. I could feel how secure he was, but it was so wonderful to hold on to my child's hand, innocent and nice, but our place was in God's House of Prayer. That made it even better to know that the love of a mother and son was with a touch of hands. As he turned to look at me, we smile and it was good and honest for both you see and we were happy as can be.

A Child's Love

A child's love is the greatest. The smile and laughter on his or her face makes the world seems a brighter place. The sounds of joy, the sadness of a cry makes us strong in every way. Dear Lord, the books, the papers and cartoon figures, all made of make believe, not yet reality. The hugs and kisses and friendly hands of course make us aware of the person we are greeting or take for granted. How wonderful is it to be living? All these things can't compare to prayers at night and good morning what's for breakfast? Oh! What a delightful sight. How often do we use these little, big words I Love You to him or her. All that come in mind are the words to remember, a child's love is important. A perfect beginning in a grown up way, the world of reality surround the newborn and become a child. With no complaints, questions or worries, with few answer to give, but plenty of advice to share. A child's love is a blessing, you bet, so keep this in mind as they grow up to be beautiful women and handsome men. Let them grow! Offspring can learn how the child's love will never die or go bye bye.

A Country Carnival Fair

Young people couldn't wait to get off the bus
Going to a sunny time fest with a crowd and long line
Look at the playground with so many things around in the area The ticket master was in the booth saying
Come get your ticket and ride
Just get one ticket or the colorful wrist band
Playing games and winning for prizes
Tasting different kinds of food
Watching the ferris wheel as it goes around
Waiting for your turn to get on and catch a light breeze
Bumping cars are fun, flashing lights, loud sound
And music playing in the place
Cotton candy and candy apples
Some caramel popcorn what a treat
You got to have something sweet
Goldfish swimming in bowls and balls to toss all over the place Get a big cold drink called the boss and then we wander on
After it is all over and it's getting late
You and others got prizes and the money is out
Our day was great and everyone got to get back on the bus
All are tired and ready to rest
Going to our location where we all started
And then we make it home
Remembering the country carnival fair
And smiling that the end we enjoy the day

A Love Song

The words are written
For all to read
Just open your mind
Let your eyes see
The true meaning of love is forgiving
Let your heart be free from all things indeed
To keep peace in order
Let your spirit be free
To wander and find everlasting destiny
In the world of many keys and different notes
Many melodies and love delights
Whisper your love song all night

A Morning Moment With My Lord

As I woke this morning and the Lord opened my eyes, I thanked him surely and went on my way, but not to sit, but to pray. I went outside and I looked around and I thanked God again for all he has done. I sang a song today and read the book, the word of the Lord. I couldn't shake it. I kept on reading and singing the songs. I hoped and prayed that my breakthrough would come. I knew in my heart that it would be soon, because there are no longer mess ups in the world that I can't come out and be cleanse. I am just here for passing and to visit a few, but wait until the big day when the kingdom comes you will be happy and joyful. Holy praise his name more than usual. I look at my past and then I go on, but I know that God is always standing by. I don't have to call him loud or soft. I call Jesus and that's enough. When things seem wrong and worrying to me, I just go off to myself and give it to Jesus and cleansing starts. So watch your ways, actions and things. Keep peace and love at the right time. Never give up and never let them down. Always remember he is around. Children are special and this is true, but give them love and it will be return to you. Amen.

Mother's Day Message
(Our Mother is Special to Us)

I haven't been here as long as my mother, but I feel I know what my mother likes and love to do. She is a special woman that God made for our family. She helped us with everything. She seen that we had food on the table, clothes on our back, learning our school work, not staying out half the night. Our mother is special and I personally want to thank God for everything you have provided for us and especially given our mother to share with us. We can say she grew up with us. The laughter, the tears and many talks through the day and night years too. She enjoyed telling us about family and we would ask questions. She would be in the kitchen or in her bedroom reading and praying about God taking care of us all, so on Mother's Day this is the message, go to your mother and hug her and tell her you love her and thanks for all she do and has done, because you only get one. So let's all enjoy the moments with mom. To all mothers young and older, Happy Mother's Day. She is your number one, that keeps the family together, so give Mom your love it means a lot and smile.

A New Day Given To Me

This is a new day given to me by my heavenly father. I rejoice in it. I will do his will and his way. I will count all my blessings one by one, and not miss none.

I look to the hills but my help comes from the Lord. I will sing songs and hymns of his glorious name, that name of Jesus. He will guide my footsteps on this day and protect me when necessary. I want to say, I love him my wonderful Father, because I know he loves me despite of the ones who dislike and want to use me. I know he will always be there with open arms and saying, "Come to me. I really care."

He woke me up this morning and I kneeled down beside my bed to tell him thank you for everything and everything is okay. Keep my mind, thoughts, heart and my soul, and my spirit under the blood, that blood of Jesus. As the day goes by, I will stop to think, I thank him every chance I get. This new day is oh so great, because my heavenly Father is always watching and willing to wait, but don't put him off. He gave us this day, okay my friend.

Old and New Collectibles

An empty, old bottle or Coke cap floating
One wheel rim and old tire that's flat
Worn out newspaper articles date back in time.
That picture frame with your sports hero or old cards.
Aged coins and homemade dolls
or photo albums with different designs on the front.
Pillow patches and used cloth from bedding to make quilts.
Those salt and pepper shakers and pot holders.
Twin sets and classy cars, all with style.
Letter writing and telephone calling that was the communication way.
Today is now and yesterday was okay,
but old and new collectibles are good,
but better than never forgetting the value of those items -
created or stored or sold.
Antiques could make you money or just keep to enjoy.
(It's yours.)

The Snow Scene

This white stuff came falling down and covered everything on the ground. It was beautiful, wonderful, cold and windy but as I see it God sent it, so things begin to happen. A man who couldn't find his way, a bird who flew along the way, a car that went off the road, a tree came crashing down with branches full of snow. It's not a lot to fuss about. Let's adjust to it. Let the kids play, the birds will continue to fly, take a brisk walk or just lay down in it and look all around and you will see a picture white as can be. A perfect snow scene, what a wonderful sight and the sun giving it plenty of light, while the snow looks really bright. Enjoy the day and try hard to make it nice.

An Old Tree

While I was waiting to leave one day
I looked out to see
A tree so bold and big
I wonder how could it be
That this tree was as tall as can be
I look from the ground to the top of the tree
What a length it had on me
A tree so long and so old facing directly in front of me
Oh what a tree
With lots of age it is old
Oh what a tree
That is big enough and not falling on me

A Young Man Goes On

He went on his way and never looked back
Took his bag and hugged and said alright
He was told take care and you can do it
A mother's love goes farther than any
Keep your head up and always grow, be strong
The days were longer and the nights lonely
But prayer was a must to get through the moments
We all were in it together from the beginning
And others were off to different locations
Some went this way, others their way
We hope he is OK at the next new station
Mother wrote letters and sent cards
We talked on the phone and laughed awhile
What happy thoughts these memories brought
Yes, you look left, then to the right
He wondered what a big life, I can make it, I will do it
Because I know who opened his hands and said you
I created, you are mine and I am yours
Keeping you safe from harm, always ok
Must believe and never doubt
God is way bigger than that, trust him, and go on
He is with you until the mission ends
Count your blessings and be humble
Praise him, praise him, he loves forever
Mom's poem for you young man, my son

A Young Man's Dream

This child that grew and grew
He was nice as can be
He had a thought that came to him
One day I will play sports
So he tried soccer of course
And got a trophy to prove it
He was good and very smart
But I pray that he keeps a good heart
Never getting mad or upset
Just do your best and it will work out
Keep the dream and that might lead him to TV
If that young man believe in himself
Oh he will go far with his dream
So keep your dream and it will one day turn into reality my son
Just wait and see
Have patience; it takes time
But always believe and you can do it

Adults Get Older

As you get older changes are showing
Your face is becoming different
Wrinkles, lines and skin getting thinner
Aches and pain come at once
Nothing that a pill or cream can't fix
Eyes are not clear and seeing at distances
Is becoming longer and making things harder
Your weight was stable
And you had energy to move along swiftly
Where is the feet for walking
My those changes have took over
Must go to the bathroom fast
Number one or two will not last
Age is only a number to most
But look at life and the body moving faster or slower
We aren't any younger
Hope for a bright day to come get out and enjoy the day
As adults we are going to need patience
And getting through our struggles
Time to meet the needs of others
All surviving children, help the elderly and the needy.

All In A Day

A mother who gets up and cooks a meal cleans the kitchen and says how are you doing? The father who goes to work and returns at three ready for dinner and a break. The brother that helps you find a toy that he lost, but not for sure. The sister who is crying and stuff, she says that's mine, be nice. The teacher who wants you to learn new skills, but you got to use your brains all in a day. The stranger that walks around, because no one seems to care. Didn't ask his name or what he's doing. The child that can't walk yet, but has a heart so big and a smile so bright it makes your day. A neighbor who brings you flowers. One person at a time turns many. Joining, sharing caring and giving and making a difference of any situation at that time. That's a clue. Why not you and others take the moment? Let us talk what great stories we all can write, working together with ideas and dreams alike. Do you wonder? We are talking good news is around us. We all hope, let's try and forget the fuss. With the right words we could unite to think about it. Please have a great day and many more to come your way all in a day smile.

Better Days Ahead For You

The office area is crowded with the curtains closed
And the windows are locked with no sunshine
The candle light is going out
Where is everybody trying to exit to
The house was still and no one moving
The wind not blowing, very silent put all on edge
You stood in one spot hope for help
Wishing for better days, but nothing came yet
Their used to be noises most of the time
Now it seems empty and trashed with bottles
Walls unpainted and broken glass
Patching holes and no water dripping
You look and see it is lonely
Will it get any better you say
From morning to night, overlooking a neon light
You think this is a messed up sight
Let it get better sooner than later
Because it really stinks
Hope for better days ahead absolutely

Break The Cycle

You probably wouldn't really think about being a baby when you were born, because everything seems normal. You didn't have a care in the world. Mother sung lullabies to you, when you began to cry. As you got older and things start to take shape, something between each parent change,teaching and talking daily helps you along the way. It was great! That makes a difference, but when things went sour you want to leave the house. I guess you could fix it and change. It is called break the cycle, turn things around, stop blaming others for your own doings and find a place in your heart for love. Take off your angry face and distrust. Make it right with smiles and laughter. Everything is not lost. Someone cares about you; godly advice is good and suggestions count. Open up and take a chance and see what good can come out. You can break the cycle. A brother, a sister or friend and a cousin unite with each other. Give a little of yourself and reach out. Everybody has feelings, emotions and most important love. You can stop hurting. Everyone has family in need, a helping hand. One word: break the cycle now. It's time.

Broken Images – but can be fixed

The person at the clearance store
They are not rich, but less than
A child without shoes
The baby that cries all night (no food)
A woman can't get her room to heat right (need to feel warmer)
The boy who hasn't eaten all night (need a meal)
A father who can't wait for his pay from last week
To provide for his family sake (take care of them)
The car that will not start (no gasoline yet)
The job you said you really like
But it was really wearing you out (no joy) just trying hard
We don't want to be broken
But come together and be fixed (in time)
It will work (hope)
No matter what your present situation
You and others can make it through
Be of good cheer
Help and be a blessing to people

Butterflies Wonderland

Many colors and beautiful as can be
Can't catch one, here comes two or three
I use a net or my hand
Those butterflies will land
For just a second you and a friend find a place to see
And have a good time with all types of species
Flying up and down all around
Now what could be more exciting then that
Giving you and I and joyful day of a scent
Smiling and anxious to see more
Looking at the butterflies that will not be missing
Because the place is so full of them
Having fun one more time and being so free
Images so created for me
Just watch them come and go
Making a picture when sitting on a rose or bush
With no one messing with them
Try not to harm them in anyway
Let those beautiful butterflies alone
All in nature that's what they are
Placed here for a reason
A wonderful combination of many colors
Keep flying and enjoying the summer

Children Our Future

Children are our future, that's what they all say. What are children without hope? Always getting messed up on dope, adults and family can't cope, so we turn to pray and get an answer from God. Help these children, show us the way. School system is failing, children in gangs, prayer is a part of it, that's right, can't win. Adults can't correct their children. The bible speak of the rod and that of God. Help the children to stay off the crack, hit the books and read the facts. Counseling needed and support groups, states raised the cost of living and children underpaid. The days are different and questionable you see, when you look at the weather what do they believe. Sun in the day and moon at night. Do they wonder about not having the light? Children having children, that's not a pretty sight. Oh, who do they think they are kidding? Education is down! Nowhere to go, no place to hide. The Lord our master is standing by. He loves the children, big and small, so find your way to Jesus. Make that your starting point. Always remember he is the beginning and the end. Never give up, he really cares. Jesus Love the little children, all the children.

Choice

Some things are little, but appear to be questioned
To define the answer is always marked
In the direction you choose to go
The future is near
As the past fades away
What is certain, and who will ever know
Your choice or my choice
Which will it be
Only God

Destiny

There is a place that has a lot of depth.
Where many memories come to the light.
For new ones and old ones that may go to this place,
will seem to wonder what's it really like.
If the time is right, then your destiny is and will be in flight.
To believe or not,
believe in the truth of the many things to dream or make real.
In the world of places to be and see, reach big
until you find an exciting destiny for thee.

Do You See?

Do you see a degree
Or a piece of blank paper to be
Do you see a rocket up there
Or a plane with a broken wing that can't fly
Do you see plants and trees or dirt
And wild roots underneath
Do you see cloud and sun light
Or rain and foggy nights
Do you see music and song
Or something off the radio station in this time
Do you see books and newspapers
Or word magazines and comic strips
Do you see the kids at play
And the babies growing without Dads
Do you see the mother that pray
And the child that wants to stay alive
Do you see the other things
That could be just for all and others like you
This is the question and hoping for answers...
We hope to find them.

Family Time Is Important

We started out with our parents and then the children came
Brothers and sisters let's remember the family
And entire generations also those close friends near and dear

Time spent and time goes on
Each other with their own, like a child, a partner or a new home We are
still family getting together
And having breakfast, lunch or dinner

Days of fun in the sun, nights out celebrating
Lots of laughter, rather playing board games or talking
Going to church events or just doing something

Family let us show love to each other from time to time
To make those memories grow even stronger
Why, because family is so very important to all
I thank God and bless families
Prayers and peace to every one, families everywhere

Fill Me Up With Good Things

Fill me up with people who love me and friends who really care.
Neighbors that take the time to greet you as they pass by.
Children who can give you a smile and a lot of laughter.
If you have patience and experiences you can make it far.

Listen to your parents. Their wisdom is great. There are stories that can't be replaced by nonsense. Always give thanks and praise for all things big and small. Gifts and talent are a blessing. Let's try to keep them forever as you live. Books to read and words to choose are as important as songs that are written.

Food and exercise are great together. That job and working are complete. Making money and having real time to create new ideas with common sense is a treat, a reward.

Protect your heart, renew your mind and watch your weight. You will be fine. One body and that's a fact. Fill me with good things and let me say thanks. Not looking back, but going forward and making it happen, that's what counts.

Find Some Good In Me

Don't go around talking this and that
Don't pick up all the mess and perhaps
Find some good in me

Don't tell lies or create a wreck
Keep on looking and want to accomplish for goodness sake
Find some good in me

Some people speak out or others may write
Some want to read others do signing which is neat
Find some good in me

They sit silent and some get louder
We feel happy and others are sadden
Find some good in me

I dream of beauty, others act ugly
He wants to drive, she wants to be a model
Find some good in me

The future is a plan to all
Joy comes with smiling more
Peace is a quiet place
Love is a heart trained and caring
Whatever you do, wherever you go
Just remember God goes with you
And he will find some good in me and you okay

First God Then Me and The Kingdom
A Growing Process
The Seed, The Plant, The Flower

The growing process first starts with a seed. Something very tiny and a little water in a special spot. Then a little tender loving care given daily as you watch it began to grow. It gets big, wide and taller it seems and branches spread out. I watch this happen and what a pretty sight. It reminded me of how Jesus wants me to grow and be. Learn and grow. I can see things better. I see beauty all over the place in my heart. The more we read the word, the more it gets down in the mind and heart, the more we will grow and grow and before we know it, Jesus is looking at us smiling and happy saying you did it. Rejoice my brother and my sister for you are in God's family, no doubt. Keep on going, don't ever stop. God is with you one hundred percent. I can make it, this I know. God said, he is with me through it all. The growing process may seem so hard, but God is always standing close by. If I care about what happens, feed the word dear Lord, that I may continue to grow and grow and between God and I he wants me to make it. This I am positive of. So move on forward and never look back. Your seed will grow into a plant and then it will be beautiful into a flower or rose or something wonderful God sent.

Friday – Step Out

We say thank God it is Friday
Let's pray and praise that day Good Friday
People like to shop and hop from store to store
Spend, spend and tell you have none
Black Friday
Someone to watch football with
Wearing purple all day waiting for Sunday
Purple Friday
Our dress wear is not that shiny
We want to put jeans on and khaki and blouses and shirts
Casual Friday
When do we get to go and eat maybe fried potatoes and fish
Fish Friday
Let's check out that scary movie, *Halloween*
No luck in that number
Friday the 13th
Watch and be quiet here comes the moment
Scream
Everyone likes Friday payday is coming
And the weekend is beginning
Enjoy your payday Friday for sure
Friday Step Out

Games People Play and Pay

A card game of some sort with spades, chess or checkers, but then people go crazy with games that cost money, like slots blackjack or dice. It all will get you much or less, so why do people continue to play all these things when people would get together and play for fun and it has become an event called gambling. When the money is gone all the paper or cards goes in the trash or leave the table, you find yourself empty-handed. What will you do next? Spend some time thinking keep doing this or quit and stop, do something better with your money. As the big board lights up or the wheel starts to spin, where will you be? Could you have helped others with their needs? Be wiser and not let the games take you under. Always remember you only you place the bet rather winning or losing. It's one thing games people play or pay. Huh! Many names for games and it might be your shame if losing everything matters.

Give A Little of Yourself

To take on a big job
To know what is right
To be kind and honest and humble
To find respect, confidence and have common sense in right or wrong
To give yourself the right push
Go ahead can mean a lot
But to take things without your control
Can lead to a lot of different problems
To help others and be yourself
You could find peace of mind
A smile that will make you feel great
Tell yourself you did a good deed for keepsake
Send flowers, write a note, send a card or just talk
That's all in giving a little of yourself

Give Us Understanding

Why do you have one hundred and thirteen people in one place And no decision can be made. A storm that was given a name, but most people homes and property are gone. The aid for help and programs not offering much, either a loan or some working with grants and hope that the paper work is correct. Do they understand or doubt the hurts? A fiscal cliff what is that? Sounds like a hill or mountain or steps to climb. Our world is upside down. We wonder what's next or going to happen in time? Let the preacher and teachers reconnect to help keep our children safe from weapons and sex. Good news, where is it now? All we get is a tv with bad news and crime. Mostly unemployment, drugs and telling lies. Wishing it would be realistic and true tides. Quick money, new cars and others crazy things, but not what we were suppose to understand. Love and forgiveness are just a few, don't forget who loves you to. Never say you are just here, there is a reason. Just remember that each year ask for understanding always and forever. Now that's a thought. Hope it gets better for each and every one that hurts. Come let's work together to make it healthier and peaceful. Are you ready? What can happen? Give, to help others daily.

God Blessings To Me

I thank you for the food we eat
I thank you for so many weeks
I pray for peace and joy and love
But most of all having true love, you Lord
So, thank you God for all you give
Not only to me, but my family so dear
Keep me from all harm and danger
Caring for me when there is no other
Just thank you dear God for everything
I haven't given my best but I pray you will
Help me complete all test
Show me what I should do
Peace be still, when storms are windy and not clear
Hold my hand, guide my steps, speak to me in the early morning Give
me courage, the ability to learn and strength to grow
A new song to sing and a pure heart alone
God blessings to me are special and very truthful this I know
God blessings are precious as gold
Everyone different in their own way
Be a blessing

God Said To Me, In A Quiet Place

To get into the kingdom you must be born again, but I ponder the thought for many things I didn't understand. I look and search for answers. I prayed. I guess that's not enough, so I must want to be spiritually change and forget about worldly and material things.

My life should be surrounded with Holy and satisfying things and not evil and corrupt ways. Lord, pick me up and place me down on solid Holy ground, for you have spoken to me. I must learn and grow in your Holy name. I thank God, the one up above who's with me from day to day for peace, love and harmony. He's spoken to me and this is what he said, "You are my child indeed. Learn to hold on to me, the one who made you and I. The one who will always be by your side. He covers and loves us all, but we must give him his honor and glory above all." I love God more because he's God.

I Cared When You Didn't
(Where were you? Let me tell you where I have been.)

Where were you when the little one came into this world, with a little blue cap and lots of baby fat? He didn't know what was going on and what was happening yet. Where were you on that special day of love, no doubt? God's gift was so precious and warm as could be. Where were you when I was placed in a room? I didn't really feel cheerful, just gloom. Where, oh where, is my baby boy? I want to hold him and until close to the morning comes. Where were you? His first steps or first tooth. What about him talking and walking to you. Where were you when he needed this man, but yet he learned dad at an old age. Where were you? Oh, did you care? Let me tell you where I have been. I was there from the beginning to the end. I saw him come into this world. He was special from day one. God gave me a son. I saw him take those steps to take a walk, go upstairs and down again. This child is laughing and not crying sadly. He has joy and gladness. This child is love and God gave him to me, to take care of and be responsible for. Let me tell you how it has been. I feel happy and filled with joy. This little one keeps me motivated. Let me tell you where I have been. I have seen him grow and grow and I hope and pray he (my son), becomes a respectful, well mannered, brave and always keeping God in his corner. He will be alright. His master really cares about him (my son) and most of all to be a good man.

Grandmom Room Has Love

Grandmom's room has plenty of love, favorite books, pictures of family and everything in place. When you enter the room say good morning and afterwards she will say, how are you and have a good day. If you feel sad, grandma would tell you come here and get a big hug. You never could come in and just go out without having a word or talking and chatting with grandmom for sure. She gives you attention from beginning to the end. Shows you love for so many. Watch as time goes by, always visit and give love to grandmom. Pray that the grandchildren grow up and do well. Older and younger trying to tell them to do their best. Grandmom you think has the questions or the answers that are sent. She gives you a smile and keeps you in mind as you go through life and enjoy the family setting and the wonderful reunion. A message for grandmom, we love you yes we do. Thanks a lot for all you do and did to make things real. We pray that this will not be goodbye or good night as you get older in age. Let us remember your wisdom and prayers. We will hold you deep in our heart and never hesitate to think of you and the room you sit or sleep. Grandmom love, oh what a room to go in and receive the love and memories each day and year.

Hair Styles Come And Go

You can have it your way with long or short quick and easy
Braid or weave different in culture
Color or no changes or stay the same
Curls or straight both will make you look great
Afro or bald from the past to the future
Fade or design cut looking good, groovy and cooler than ever
But all this is OK - just get some hair and weave
Or your own with a style
Some get wigs and then there are twists
Whatever you prefer will be the style you wish
Your hair is your own to take care of
No matter how you decide to wear it
No wave, extensions, hot combs, rollers or just press or afro Enjoy and
feel good about yourself wearing any style
Remember hairstyles come and go for all people
For adults or children
Styles your way

Happy Birthday Friend

You are middle-age, wearing glasses and forgetting things
Your sense of humor makes me laugh
Traveling is your thing, but money can go fast
Your family is so big
I hope your birthday is exciting
Because something or someone should make you happy
Blow out the candles on your cake and don't drink too much
Enjoy yourself and have some fun
Remember you will not see this one anymore to come
You are getting older now
Hope you realize you are not twenty-five anymore
God bless you on your day
Take time to pray for many more your way my friend
You know when you had enough
Go relax and think about all the stuff
That made you happy and full of life
Watch your time go by
Can't go back or look behind
The moment is yours to un-rewind
Meet and greet your guest
Hope you get what is best
It's your birthday
Sing and enjoy the rest

Have A Good Day

The reason may not mean everything to you
But pray anyway read the word
Invite yourself to a cup of coffee or tea
Take a warm bath or go to the spa for free
Wear your favorite colors or lounge in matching set of pajamas
Get the morning going scan the newspaper or the funnies
Read a good exciting book of mystery or recite poetry
Walk a short distance with a friend or family member
Ride a bicycle but take it slow and be careful
Send some little items to a needy person or relative help them
Check the mail and get those ads
Go on the Internet for a while but remember watch your time
There is more to do cut some flowers
Make a nice dinner
You might have company
Play with the pet that you just met
Mother is calling return the call
She got recipes to make a cake or homemade pies
Move on, look forward, keep praying for others who are sick
Show some kindness in your heart
Oh and have a good day
Because you never know how many more will come your way
We hope many

Here I Am

I waited day and night to talk. You said meet me here, but you were busy and didn't care. I look over here and I went there. Your friend and family try to find you. Where? You left this note. What was the message? Your phone is off and your writing is imperfect. What do you want me to do? I try so hard to get by, but I got pushed into this lie. Help, before it's too late. God is telling you to wait, here I am come to me, find your life in peace, rejoice and humble yourself. Just talk to me. Here I am my friend. Bless you for coming my way. I can show you goodness and faith, clean you up and make you whole, turn your wrongs to right, pray morning, noon and night. Remember me, here I am always.

If I Ever Tell You

If I ever tell you to be quiet
It was because I wanted you to listen
If I ever cried around you it was because I care
If I ever tell you I love you
It was the truth and not a lie
If I ever tell you to be strong
It was because I believe in you
But to pray and be thankful means a lot more
So I shouldn't ever have to tell you
Because both of us all of us know
God is always near to lend his divine ear and hand
If I ever tell you
Just remember I did tell you

How To Help One Another

It could be a little change
Or maybe just a smile to take away the pain
You can help a neighbor out or walk along and talk
You can visit the children site or find a friend you like
You can read to little ones are just help to care and that's a lot Always be kind and very nice
You see, God is looking and very pleased
How to help one another
Just try to learn to listen and listen to learn is the real key
May we care and not turn our backs
Someone help us and that's a true fact
Never look down on the other
You and I are really no better just trying to live
Find a life of comfort without destruction
But more holy instruction
How can one help each other
Try God and he will give you the rest of the plan to follow
Believe in yourself and share it with someone
Who needs hope and justice

I Am Not Alone Never

Pray God Heals Me

On December 27, 1997, I was taking my family to our old community and all of the sudden I got a sharp pain that I couldn't shake. I told my mother about this pain and the closer we got to the town the worse it got, so my mother told me to go to the place where my aunt and uncle were so I did and the pain was still there. I went to the room and fell against the wall and proceeded to go to the bathroom area, but my aunt told me that they were going to pray for me and anoint me with oil and I was sitting in a chair and my Mother, my Aunt and Uncle prayed for me, calling on the name of the Lord and I was crying and my Aunt touched me in the painful area and I was praying God and thanking God, saying hallelujah and I didn't feel no more pain, so I knew I was not alone. God was right there with me and bringing me through having faith and trusting in God brought me through it all. Three or more gather together in the name of Jesus. With Jesus in my life I can do all things through Christ who strengthens me. Christ is all I need, that wonderful name of Jesus. This is a true story.

I Cried To My Jesus
(My Time)

I woke in the morning and I was sitting down on the bedroom floor. I was recording a gospel song and as I was listening to the song, it was "I Will Not Complain" and the more I listened, I began to cry and as I cried more and more, I got down and was on my knees and I was praying to Jesus and I got louder and louder, lifting my hands and still crying. I felt a big relief come over me. I was sweating all over my body. I felt it dripping off of me. I knew that Jesus was with me. I loved what was happening. I believe in Jesus and even though I was in the house by myself, I was not alone at all. He was just waiting for me. I needed him and he came to me. I told him, thank you and continued to give him his praise. Jesus cares about me and this I know. I love to say Jesus, because I know that name has power. I will not complain, because Jesus takes care of his own.

I truly believe
Thank you Jesus
King of Kings
Lord of Lords
Jesus Loves

This is the day that the Lord has made. I will rejoice and be glad in it.
Psalm 118-24

I Said A Prayer For You

I said a prayer for you
That was heavy on my heart and mind
I hope you hear it Lord
For it's about my son
I love him because he is a gift from you
But Lord I hope his guardian angel is always near
That people will not try to hurt him and make his little life a mess
But God I know you are with him until eternal life
I care about him dearly and hope the best for him
That's why I said a prayer today
Especially just for him
Oh father in heaven
You are number one
Keep my son in your great big hand
Hold him tight and never let go
Lord I ask that you let him grow
To be the kind of person that's wise and with an honest soul
Keep the faith that he has
And hold onto the written true word (The Bible)
And when you Lord speak to him
Let him hear and learn from you
This is my prayer I said today
Amen thank you Jesus

Smile Just For A While

A smile will make you happier during the day
Your face lights up like sunshine
Don't waste your time frowning, it will not get you where you are going
Take time to smile
People will always wonder why you are so happy
Better things should come your way by smiling
Joy and full of life, smile it is nicer
Gee, just do it and see
Smile, smile and watch the crowd
Somewhere inside of you hoping to come out
Stop pressing it in, that's no fun
Look in the mirror and practice your grin
The expression can be great
But smiling is so wonderful and beautiful
That comments keep coming
You never know who will tell you they like your smile
I love it
Don't stop and you'll start laughing ha ha

If You Leave

You will be missed and hope not to cry
With my emotions from you and I
My arms stretched out for a hug and good-bye
Our moments were good, the talks were pleasant
Why do I feel so awkward
I need to say this and hope you are happy for us
But if you leave, remember one thing
Our hearts did beat as one
Take time to think of all the precious things
And the places we shared
You shared them with me, your baby, your boo
Keep the faith and let's move on
Our yesterday's tomorrow's are gone
The future looks bright
And let's always leave by saying or doing things right
If you ever leave, just say a prayer that both can really enjoy
With mostly love and no regrets
We will learn to forgive but not forget

In The Mood
(Passion)

Let us come together as we look at each other
With no drama or unspoken words
Bring yourself to the moment of truth
And see what will be or wonder, can say or do
Imagine this time so free
Open your eyes to what is in front of you
A woman of color with character and expression
And loving and kind trying to keep important things in line
What do you see in this lady, who do you want her to be
Like your mother or just be her, your queen
The man that is chosen, strong, protected
And speak well to many all about his business
God has blessed him and willing to help
Have a good heart and enjoy outside activities of some sort
Music as smooth jazz or a summertime breeze night
He looks excellent to be with or king of his place
The mood is right, the two hope it works out
Enjoy the pleasure of it all
In the moonlight setting, the place is gorgeous
You and someone special
Your queen fulfilling each with passion and humble beginnings
In conversations, a few hugs, holding hands and some kisses
The rest of it is romantic, in a unique way, Oh! (so good)
We enjoy in the mood and the moment made for two
But do not take the time for granted
You and your queen will lose it
Both keep the passion flowing

In The New Year

Let's move, ladies.

We deserve the best time ever, so I'm starting and finishing points. Take in the movies or a gospel music celebration or a play or family fun. Get your beauty back and try to lose some weight you must take care of yourself and maybe Mr. Right will find you. In the new year go to school, take some classes or write a book. Get it now. Go on the journey and refresh your mind and time. Keeping your finances and not messing it up with wasteful things. Curb your spending, have fun on the beach or on the sand. Let your lifestyle change for the better. Focus daily and watch your thoughts and words out of your mouth. Skip the past photos and the old news. Find a friend who really cares and spends time and getting to know each other and maybe it will last a while and don't forget to smile. Enjoy and have fun even if it doesn't last or work out. Just thank the one anyway for all the times spent and move on all not lost. (Keep moving.)

Inside or Outside of You

Search inside of you and find the better things to do
There is love, kindness, honesty and a pure heart
But on the outside your problems start fear
Not being optimistic, confident low
Patience thinning, experience not that great
You're hiding place isn't working out
The shield or guard wasn't protecting you anymore
All that comes out is ugliness and loneliness
You desire to believe and hope
But diligence must be better or else
Stay steadfast and learn the true meaning of faith and hope
You have it within, but bring it to the surface
To the outside isn't easy
Will you be ready from the inside out
Watch, watch wait and see
What will be for you or any other (searching you)

Inspired To Be People

A person or people that you know what to do
In a society made up of you and me
Our names are different, tell no history to define us or shape one
Or the other mind they said all are in it together
When we try to do right and keep inside the rules that are set
The changes come to be something else
Our ancestors prayed, talked and sung songs to comfort us
And gave their lives for us
Wake up people of color and dig deep in your soul
There's a new generation arising
And need our help to compete to complete what we see today
And in the future, destiny in every way, hope for living
Not in a world that's not giving but taking
By so many crazy and corrupt ways
That actions are totally no good with people who will not believe
But likes to fulfill greed and that's not the answer we need
Where is peace and harmony

Judge Yourself Not

You will make mistakes and fall but, look at it all
God sees and is always willing to forgive big or small
Wait and see what God can do
There is hope and be kind and sweet
Humble yourself and never look down
Have faith and keep love around
A merry heart and character delight
Be glad and rejoice and shout it's alright
Judge yourself not
Watch how you act
Speak slowly and listen well
Nobody has anything pleasant to say
Then don't take it in your circle, ok
Keep your face, eye and a smile
Everything will get better by and by
Your soul cries mercy on me
And help give everlasting love from above, believe
Root and ground me and fill the emptiness
With knowledge and understanding for yourself
Peace, promises and praise
The three P's that make up for the rest of it
Please don't judge yourself yet
Wait, wait and see

Lend a Helpful Hand

Faith and truth are important, treasure
Prayers and rejoice will make it better
Lend a hand, yours
Ideas and skills, your goals to keep unwanted problems out
Pushing forward to those dreams career bound
Take those unused coins and turn them into dollars
Help someone else along the way, who needs money
When the doctor did house calls and mid-wives helped
Mother and babies now it's different
Doctor appointment and physician assistance
And all the health information on computers
You paid just a little cost back then in the era
But now things are higher
Clothes with tags in the closet and shoes not being worn
Lend a hand to help others who are wanting
They can really use them
Coupons and stamps for food and milk
Water and sewer are not free
Socks and warmers will help your feet
Those gloves for your hands
Coats and jackets can keep you warm for the body during winter
Blankets and spreads, hold onto the other items to share
You all can smile
Trees and flowers in the yard
Hopes for spring and summer not to fly
Pets and animals are ok to care for
Don't leave them hungry and scared
Gas, oil or electricity and wood are used
But matches, lighters or battery flashlights are good to have
For a back up supply
Cold or hot, rather Alaska or Arizona
Check it out, so pick one you like
Lend a helpful hand
A trip to travel, where you've never been
Picture it

Life

L is for learning, love and likable ideas with lessons
I is for if all things are possible (receive)
F is the future and what it hope for
E is everything can be beautiful for eternity
Don't take life for granted
Enjoy it the right way
The holy way
God's way with your heart and soul in it
Check yourself
It is your life to choose to go in the right direction
Or go down the dangerous highway
The sign reading a dead end
You make your mind up all on your own
Then you will see where you came out right or wrong
That's life

Morning Dew

As I look out the window everything is dew, the grass every object in sight. The wet look is everywhere, with the sunshine peeking out. Can I come on out? You see, my name is Morning Dew. I am an early morning delight. What might yours be? Mr. Sun of course, that is me! I give light. Like one, two and three all day long I shine. You see, no one can replace me not even you. Mr. Dew or whoever you want to be, I will just remain as a wet look dew. I am comfortable with you. Have a good day, Mr. Sun. Keep your light for everyone and I will keep my Dew for morning blues.

Lift My Voice

God I want to sing for you, but I need your guidance to do it. Oh, God help me to be the one chosen to sing from my heart and not just my mouth. Oh, let my voice be lifted and heard all over the place. Let my voice be strong and great. I lift my voice to him, the Creator, the Savior, and for all in Heaven. Lift me up dear lord that all my singing, all can make it. All those voices lifting the name of Jesus up higher and higher. God first all the time, so we must sing praises right now. Oh lift my voice. I am ready again and again.

Lord What Do I Do?

I love my son and must raise him. I love my mother if she wants to move to a new location. Oh, Lord what do I do? I pray about this situation, but I feel like I should be doing something not nothing. Help me dear Lord, to go forward and not look back, because new things should happen and old things are gone out. What do I do in time? I need help. I go to the solid rock and pray and ask my Father in Heaven, for which he is a great listener, and then and only then I will get my answer. Help me to see what I am doing wrong. Help me to make it all right. Keep my head up and my mouth filled with the word and not things of this world. Help me to keep my feet firm on the ground. Just pray for comfort, joy and peace and always remember that God is always there to extend a helping hand. I call upon the name of Jesus who will supply all my needs. I am blessed, so truly blessed. Let my light shine before my enemies, my family and friends, my brotherly love, brothers and sisters. Amen.

Magic Moment In The Air

The picture is set
An ocean wave
Sand under your feet
A blanket for the picnic
And a basket with lots of food of every sort
It is getting late and the mood changes to a quiet peaceful still night
You can hear the waves on the beach
You and I try to keep warm and not chill or catch a cold
The place is awesome and the company is delightful
But we wish it could go on and on
But we must come back to ourselves
And find a minute together, who we really are
Take some time and try to visualize all the wonderful things
Each of us could be creating and no regrets to talk about
Treat yourself and me as a man and woman who cares
Mostly everything and not just anything
We can make it, if you really care
Are we willing to go there, in the magic moment in the air
Wishing

May I

May I tell you about the gift of life
True comfort and blessings and more delight
All the great works in the air, the sea and in the land
We get snow, rain and the wind and an awesome sun
Creations in different places
Birds find their own feeding
I heard a voice singing in love and praises
A believers ear wants to hear about hope and peace everywhere
You are never by yourself
I must tell you, prayer is talking to the Almighty God
So pray, hold onto his powerful hands
Faith is believing and not giving up for a moment
May I tell you something wonderful
Thy will be done on earth and in heaven
I can tell you thank you for birth, middle age and senior living Show
your mercy and kindness to your children
Throughout those generations
May I close with prayer
And love of family, life and your beautiful thanksgiving
Bless all just say....may I

My Brother and a True Friend

He came into the house of the Lord
And sat as still as he could be
But down in the same aisle his mother, sister
Uncle and nephew were sitting and delightful to see him
On such a special day for mothers, you see

He looked, he watched and he slept
But when the big moment came to go to the front of the church He
stood and they reached for his hand and called out
Come to Jesus, do you know him yet, one on one
That personal view to you

But nothing happened, not this time
But surely there will be another one
That's my brother, not willing to give in yet
One day he will not come as a guest, but he will pass the test
Let him join the family, the ones that are Christ like and Holy
For sure now, forever and always and more

He stood up, he walked out
What joy did he miss doing that
Prayers going up, songs being sung
Thank you Lord for everything, that you have done
Let your will and ways help bring this brother back home
And meet a true friend who will be there even at the very end

Keep your peace, never give up, let the Lord work
Bring it all to pass and he will rejoice all nights
Because you can't hide from the light
Let it shine, let it shine my brother, now is the time

My Heavenly Father vs The Earthly Father

When my heavenly father created, the earthly father was well and was placed over all things of the Earth. My heavenly father was in the giving business, while the earthly father was receiving all things possible, but one day the earthly father got greedy, because his wife insisted they eat the fruit from the special tree, not given to him to touch. The earthly father always wants things he can't have or afford, but because he sees it, he got to have it or touch it, some of the time. My heavenly father is understandable. You ask questions and you get answers. Never quick to shut you out, without helping the situation first or right on time. Then the earthly father ideals of living changes, also, his ways of thinking and character, his different behavior and attitude towards things and situations. My heavenly father still remains the same in the present and the future events taking place. My heavenly father cares about you and what happens to all remember that he loves you. The earthly father can do some things or nothing. My heavenly father can do all things. The earthly father love is more of a likeness. My heavenly father is all about love. The earthly father can make disappointment happen. My heavenly father has encouraging ways to help us. The earthly father can leave you all alone. My heavenly father is always there. My heavenly father knows what's best. The earthly father tries his best and forgets the rest. With my heavenly father you can live with him always and forever. With your earthly father it is only a little while, not forever and surely not long. My heavenly father provides a wonderful holy life and a kingdom home worth living in. The earthly father dreams of a house, he can't call his home. Not a lot of love is in his life. It's temporary and it's not going to always be there or maybe last. My heavenly father is a guaranteed father and the earthly father, Pray to not be a part time, but full-time father or daddy. Where is he? How do I find him? Does he love me or does he really care? My heavenly father is waiting on you to call him and come to him. Call his name and my heavenly father always sees and listens. My heavenly father had the word from the beginning. The earthly father words are made up as he goes along. My heavenly father stands right beside you and me and every time he carries us along the way all day. The earthly father sits and stands and sometimes doesn't know where to be found. My heavenly father is always willing and caring about everyone and what's going on. The earthly father is supposed to be learning and mostly forgetting and sometimes unforgiving and has lost hope of needing and caring about others, mostly his children. Your choice, your life, your fathers, your answer. Who is your father in life? God gave example.

Jesus Build A Fence Around Me

Jesus build a fence around me from my enemies
Protect me when I go out and when I come in
If I go here and there and everywhere
Let me know that my fence is there to protect me
From all these corrupt things of the world
Let there be peace, joy, love, meekness and rejoicing
In whatever things I'm doing for you
My fence will be strong, sturdy and to be able to withstand all
That comes my way why, because I know that Jesus Christ is
With me all the days of my life and eternally, that's why

My Letter To You And Only You

I am not perfect. I have made mistakes, but God you have been there to pick me up. How can I not know you? For you are always there, if I just took the time to notice my quiet time with you. I have come a long way since then. I really know you were there for me. I love to know you and how happy I am. I just enjoy that inspiration. All that are against me, you dear Jesus is always standing by, closer than a brother, smarter than a sister, learning more than a mother, but you are greater than a father. I really like my new life with you, but I must let you take full control of my life and to love others. Help me to make it in this progress. That at the end, I will be your good and faithful servant. Always giving you your honor and glory. You are the alpha and omega. You are Jesus Christ, my supplier, protector, healer, lawyer, doctor, judge etc. Jesus is the one for me. He cares about me and he is all I need. Give me understanding of your word.

Love
Believe
Faith
Hope
Eternal Love

My Welcome Place

As I was looking toward the dining area
I noticed that the sun was shining bright through the window
I say to myself it is time for me to spend time
With my friend Jesus and the word of truth
I sit down in my favorite chair next to the window where the light was
I felt good about it and warm
It was like Jesus gave me a big hug and said good morning
I asked Jesus to take me through and order my steps along the way
I got a friend and what a friend indeed
I know he is all ways right there for me
Sometimes I talk out loud to my friend
And sometimes I just whisper to be heard
Thank you friend for a lovely day
Thank you for my welcome place to stay and I know I can visit anytime
But you just bring to my attention, the warmth and sun
My welcome place is special to me
No one can take it away from me
It may not be special to others
But I will always know it means a lot to me
And I can come no matter what
You are there Jesus and time is truly spent
My welcome place is important to me

Myself

What is it really like to know me? What are you really about? I ask myself, who am I? What can I do to make things smooth and with ease? I will be an achiever, keeping my name, or a leader or I am just plain old myself and living with me. What will the future really be? I am quiet, sometimes moody, very helpful and always reading. A peacemaker of some sort wanting to be more or not, just alright and don't want to face anymore. Help me Lord to see, what plan you have for me. All I want is to be myself and especially me.

Never Feel Alone

As I sit by myself and wonder and meditate, I feel occupied with many thoughts. Some are good and some are bad and some are weak. I feel to be never alone as long as my friend is near. He helps me through the day and gives me rest at night. I will never be alone. I can talk to my friend. I listen with open ears. I will never be alone. We are close and separating is none, so pray for me my friend, because we will never be alone. My friend cares for me. He stays all around me. You see I never feel alone, because my friend is there watching over me you see.

Never Let A Day Go By

To say I care about you my child
Love is a powerful word for sure
Your most wonderful meaning of together is kindness
It is not a secret formula but reality

Try to keep yourself and people you meet in time
Traveling or walking along and forming friendships or relationships
Last in that place or countryside

Never let a day go by
Stop fighting and violence is not the answers
Old times neighbors share and say good morning
Are these days really over
How amazing it will be if real people who came before us
And apply knowledge and skills to problems of today

Take a look and see what works or are we doomed
Where is the good instead of the bad
Read from your Bible and read the word
There is a story for all to maintain and read it again
The answers are there that's a promise from God
Never let a day go by that is for you and I
Let's all try
It started from the beginning

Never Too Busy For God

We always rush from here to there
Never really going or doing anything so important to spare
But morning and noon it is time to go to God for everything
He just wants us to care about him as he cares about us
Never Too Busy For God
Look at yourself and check yourself
Who am I
What am I doing
Can I do it alone
But Never Too Busy For God
Go to him
He is waiting for you or us
So teach me God not to be so busy that I don't come to you
In the morning and late in the evening to show you that I care
But you care for me
I am asking you to help me
Not to be so busy that my day isn't wasted
Or spend time with no meaning
But God gave me this day
So I will not be too busy to spend time with you
Stay for awhile
Listen to my instruction
I got to hold on, pray and seek you until I see you again
You are my savior, my rock
And no one can be so busy that they can't come to the creator
We all belong to you
Never Too Busy For God
Take care of me
I need you more than anything
Stay with me
Help me and others too
God loves his children

Noon and Night

In the day at twelve noon that's prayer and thanking God. Time to express how much you love and understand prayer and promises of God. Then comes the night you pray that all will be alright the family, friends, the community and the president in command, all the kids in every school, the teachers, the store owners, the business representatives and bankers and loaners, but at the end of the day we want to thank God. For all these words are connected. They are saying something, adding just more. You make that decision between noon and night. Fold your hand and speak or close your eyes and just go to sleep. That's the solution. Your precious time counts on both of these right now, more than ever not of your leisure.

One on One
(The Game)

One on one, you call basketball
I take you there, you spot me five
The ball is mine and the goal is high
Shoot it, but the game is not over until the clock goes to zero
My shot counts and now you want a rematch
Try me later without the others
They cheer you on the court
You twist and spin and no foul called
I made one basket and you closed your eyes
My hand goes up and you made it, how lucky right
But at the end we still want to win
So two people and the final play or game likes to play one on one
All over again the game goes on, one hopes to win

Now I See With Years Moving On

Now I see that little toddler is grown
Now I see that little boy who name is not chunky
Now I see a bigger child smiling
Who loves to look at TV and plays sports
And Mom cares more about homework
Now I see the look in his eyes, smile on his face, laughter when we play
Now I can see him reading the Bible book and helping out in church
I can see pictures from a baby until now
Lots of memories to be found
I can see him singing a song or riding his bike
Or just messing with plastic army men and making wrestlers fight
I can see him building his body and running real fast
I can see him getting his grades and saying yes
Now I can see what God blessed me with
To learn him the true way and repent
I now see my work is cut out for me
But with faith and lots of prayers God is right by your side
Son as you get older and become a young man
Just remember your heavenly father is keeping you straight and live,
You cannot do it all by yourself
Smile, one day you will say now I see Mom helped by God
Put God first ok
Thank God first in all that you do

Ocean Blue

Let's go where the water flows
Sometimes high and sometimes low aquamarine clear and cool Oh, but
what a ocean so big and blue
Is this really true waves of water coming toward the shore
My what a wonderful ocean to explore
Many sea shells, sea creatures and lots of sand
When you go out to the ocean
Ask God to hold your hand
Ocean, big, ocean blue why is that color so brightly seen
Feeling warm as you can see and where you really want to be
But take your time and walk, talk, laugh and enjoy it all
Because there is peace in the midst of it all
On the bright colorful ocean blue for you and yours
And all to enjoy a place that many go and find excitement
And happy moments and memories alike just find
Some time, blue ocean scene

The Best and the Worst Times

You took her on her first date excited (Best)
Oh I got there but was late (Worst)
Parents told you have her home at a certain time
And you reply I will and did (Best)
You told her that you got to make a stop and time going on
We got to go and then you didn't care about the time
Or what the parent said next (Worst)

Sports and different activities were important
But you took the time out to tell her to try harder and she will make it
(Best)
Your sports and events mean a lot to you
So you played them all the time
And you called her and you didn't make time for her (Worst)

Graduation was coming and everyone was happy
They clap and cheer as each pass by to receive their diploma
They deserve it (Best)
You came up short and didn't want to participate
In the most rewarding event of the year
What happened you got all incompletes in all the classes you said you
like (Worst) Best is good and worst can be awful if you let it

On This Day, The Reason Our Lord

We do all the trimming of the trees and our homes. Eat plenty of food, give out lots of gifts, spend lots of money, but do we remember the reason of holiday season. It is about our Lord, the one who created heaven and earth to celebrate his birth and his coming. We are his people and we need to pray and ask for forgiveness. Learn to love one another, caring and sharing and keeping the hope, faith and believing and keep his name forever and look to the almighty victory day of rejoicing and singing with our Lord and Savior. That's the reason for this holy season. Let us remember. Let us not climb in the hills, but look to the hills with cometh our help from the Lord in our glory hallelujah on this great day that the Lord has given us. Praise his holy name. The name above all names. Love be to our Lord. Praise always and forever. You are kings of kings.

One Man Dream

A man born in a small town decided to branch out to go far.
Sometimes to different cities and states not wondering his faith. Would he be successful or not move in on his own selling items and passing on information to others hoping everything would come together. When or wherever does he want to be wealthy or is it avoid he's trying to replace or feel thinking bigger and getting emptier. You can't take your treasures with you. Is this a journey or dream for nothing or a passion my friend, one man traveling up-and-down in time. Got a plan or a wasted mind filled with unpopular moments and disappointments and a lot of drama. So let's try to live and love. That's a lot to his family, friends and others who can help. Your dreams enjoy the journey you have chosen.
Wait patiently from God and pray you can make it.
After all your one man dream is exciting and lively.
Wishing for a good fortune.

One Girlfriend Wishes

A bunch of roses in a designer clear vase
The ring that is big as the diamond rock
All the gifts that he wrapped
Are sitting waiting to be attacked by her
His apology will it mean something
The love letters that you written
Did you keep one for something
Words in the car came straight from the heart
We said compliments long overdue
Did it show anything different to you
He got on one knee and begged please come back baby to me
You asked did I need money or a meal
He tried to offer to pay my bills
But she just want to be
To take care of things her way or say nay, no not me
Hope she would give him some time
And she probably would change her mind
She really looks good
He replies he thinks about the future
Oh God one place they both remember
Can they keep it flaming when romancing and dining
The life we plan together
It will be amazing again and making it forever
She wishing

One Man Outlook On Life

The man remembers how young, vibrant he used to be
So cool and very natural dress down from head to toe
Oh his shoes had a glow
He would be walking straight up without a care in the world
Not really wondering about a girl
His time for now
As he got older some things began to happen
Mishaps and falling
The image of the man had changed
His words were slower and his walk not so fast
Sitting and thinking what is happening
His hair was grayer and so was his beard
I changed to an old man
It felt like a minute
My view of me what will it be
Or am I looking forward to seeing my outlook here and now
Rather young or old
Help me through this life of mine
The outlook of the man

One Separate Him or Herself with the Holy Book

The Bible

He or she sits off to himself with the Bible at their side, with pen in hand and paper to write all the principles of the good book, what it's about.

He speaks no words. It shows on their faces. He's really into this great text you see.

The author is true. The words is his own. He writes and reads that wonderful message. Oh, how it seems at that moment a place, a space to call his own.

The words jump out at you. The book is big and many wonder what makes it so unique and antique. That is one that can't be beat, not now, not then and not in the future. One of a kind, if we only apply it to our lives. This great book, the Bible, we are separate for a reason. A peculiar people who enjoy and appreciate the great book that's written.

Open the Window, Close the Door

The morning mist on the window frame
Fresh air in the springtime
A cool chill day and brisk weather to be
Just think of the sunflowers, roses and different plants
Made for a bed of wonderful scents
Do you open the window or just keep it shut
A new beginning is great
A closed window is absent from the world
Never knowing what could be out there
Shut the door and stay a while
Find a good book or just reading the papers
A cup of tea or a funny comedy on TV
Focus on the views of the things
That have meaning and not the blues
Reflect on the ideas that will come your way
Let's open our windows to release a new possibility to come
Start today at this moment in time and the present
Giving you insight that can be so loving
Keep living

Original People In Different Places

Not about color nor our names
Just plain people in different places
We have cultures and customs
Some have houses and others mansions
Books are written and newspapers are now digital
Times not waiting and the currency is changing
Get your diploma keep pushing for your degree
And hope for a job at the best level
Women think bigger and men are getting greedy
No word spoken little children laughing not crying in the street They want playgrounds and sweets
People are trying and we need to be loving
And forgiving to each other and stick together
Let's try harder at caring and not be so empty
Original people just want to make it
Rather here or other places
We are people

Pain

Most can be hurt or be torn,
By the anger, disguise or temper in all of us,
But to feel that awful sign or symptoms is all but to great,
For all who come in contact with this one.
We all keep facing the jaws of this on and off effect of the simple word –
(Pain)

Our Thanks For God's Blessings

God thank you for life, family, health
And daily feeding of your word day and night
That turns into weeks to make years
We pray for your love, joy and peace
But most of all having true love, your love
So thanks for all you give, not only to us
To families so dear, keeping us from harm and danger
Caring for all and many others afar
Thanks for the good times and bad
Sometimes we don't give our best
But prayer and hope help us not take things for granted
Each should try to complete the test
That applies to everyday living, be positive
God always shows us what to do
Gives us comfort when storms come our way, wisdom
A new song to sing, the awesome praise to him from within
Teach the little ones to pray, be blessed with every new day
For God loves forever and never fails
So remember, thank you God

Over Here Over There

Valentine special, birthday party
Roses, jewelry, balloons spending for everything
Cookies, candy, sweets, sugar and sexy items
To whom they belong, a date or a mate
That will create a lovely time and shows good manners
And wonderful taste that follows you
Wear your finest attire at the birthday party

Red for the ladies and all want to go the Valentines dance
And an awesome dinner for two at their favorite restaurant
Watch the couples come together to make things happen
Feeling love and appreciated, that's the secret of real love
And one day turning into marriage just know what you want
And working at it until that time comes to be one
Do you get it, will not happen overnight

Happy Valentines and birthday to all and enjoy the evening
At least no one is lonely, hope all goes well and with a smile
And it will be special to the one you love or have
Keep an open mind and heart, so that magic can bring
You a lifetime partner that they may arrive some day
And make you very special in every way
Full of love perhaps be happy, put these days together
And wait and see what can be now and forever

Paths That Cross

A Friend, A Stranger, A Child or Just Me

There you are
Haven't seen you for awhile, my friend
I caught a glimpse of you just as you went by
And didn't get your name, a stranger
I saw a little one laughing and smiling today
My what a wonderful child
I talked to someone who told you
That they want to speak just to me and be with me always
And I want to know who it was
And what his or her name was
And I found out his name was
Wonderful, marvelous, glorious, majesty
It was Jesus, that's the good shepherd
The Lord of Lord
Jesus is our hope

Peace/ Pain/ Place/ Pray

There was peace on that day
Was peace of going to a routine job, running errands
Or just getting on the plane, caught the school bus or just touring

Then there was pain
All came to a halt and the buildings collapsed
Planes taken out people, fighting for their lives
Smoke and dust everywhere, people screaming
Ambulance sirens, firemen and policemen
Scrambling to make sense of such a heartbreaking event in the city
Helping each other to recovery

We know the place New York, large huge and lots of people
Taxi cabs and buses and cars and trucks everywhere
In this big city, two towers tall as could be
Why would terrorists do this to them
The place must be built and renewed and make some changes
Keep the faith and never give up
God is in control and that's a fact

Let us pray, trust and believe God is the answer
Indeed, we always see God Bless America
But let's turn around and American should be blessing God
For all he created all that he will do and have done
Let's all say amen and thank you Jesus
He paid the awesome price
That's what we all should be united and love
And care for one another, that would be best.

Phone Call Classic

Hanging on the phone line sitting or waiting for it to ring
The phone different kind of position
We can't keep still, don't know who listening
Time is winding up, just a few more minutes
You wish it could continue on, but that cost money and isn't free
Rather you talk now or some other day, you try to get your phone call in
Don't let the call be long, never know when it will end
Your minutes are ticking away
Should I keep talking or just give in
Before I do hear a dial tone or the phone goes dead
How long will it take to place a phone call from here to there
Waiting seems like it takes forever
Everything is high-tech using cards instead of cents
Got to go for now I will check back later
Or voicemail or something or hope for a text saying hello or goodbye all
on a call What happened to talking face-to-face
That was the best

Pittsburgh Steelers Come Back

The team that was great in black and yellow has faint into less than any. The last Super Bowl was a long time ago. The coach is angry and mad, get it together. The quarterback can't decide to make a change. He blames it on the new rules of the game like Pop Warner: you can't hit too hard. The team is not together, running around like a bee. The scoreboard tells the story. The home team fans aren't coming to wave their towels or wear an outfit they like in their colors. Where are the Steelers at the mill or on a vacation at this point? What is the deal? Some say get it right or pack your bags and call it a night. The year is not going your way, regroup and try harder. Keep what you want, but let go what you may. Just get us a winning team in 2015. Hurray! Good luck, but please get out of the rut. Shut it down and stop acting like clowns. We want a team that's strong. Winning games is a must. You are the home team forever.

Pray For Us To Be Happy

Come, let us bow our heads as we speak to the Almighty God. Pray that we come together as one with love, joy, happiness and peace to fill our lives. Anyone that is going to enter into our circle of the family, may they be blessed and the new little ones that will arrive. Keep us in unity. The right matter, as we take care of work time, business and play and appreciate all the movement with each other. May it be safe and carefully done to enjoy the activities, watching and waiting for the new experiences and different events. The doors that open and the ones that closed. Always help us to pray and keep a sweet and humble melody in our hearts, to take out all the world trials and upsets. Love is so important. Take each season and make something beautiful from it. Help us Almighty God with all understanding of love and patience, that we can stand. If we must go out, cover us with your armor to survive all the things of the wilderness and let us pray for all and they pray for us too. May God bless all with belief and hope and cherish the moments of a wonderful love, happiness always and forever. Be happy and enjoy one to another. Pray for us.

Press On, Your Needs Will Be Met

Press on in this world of ours
While plants animals and places are changing rapidly
Water not that great lakes and rivers frozen
Causing everyone a headache soon it will be over
Eating the same old foods and scared
To try something new and exciting
Electric and gas very high and winter is really hitting us hard
People still go out and get bread eggs and milk
Some stores are closing and we will have to go a little farther
Oh what's the matter tired of driving
They tell us to leave the sugar alone
But most everything has it what do we do ignore it
We pray that all will be alright
Because spring is around the corner don't quit
Summer isn't far behind with warmer temperature and beaches
Swimming and wearing our sunglasses no wait awhile
Let's just breathe because it is coming real soon
Just be ready my friend your needs will be met
You'll see

Run Children Run

How many do we know like this? Children who get up and on the go. From sunup to sundown, they probably have made it across cities and towns. Drinking here, smoking there, telling lies, cussing and stealing in their styles. Where do they run? Where do they go when it is all over? Where do they really end up in a prison cell or six feet under? Shouting and swearing this and that. Rapping negative stuff like that. They all need help from the one up above, because family members have tried and cried and no one else can handle it. It's too painful to bear, not pleasant to see these run children run are running free. No curfews, how do you do it all tell you I don't care what you do in the neighborhood. We need good role models for the young ones to bring them upright, the best we know how. Oh! Daddy, Daddy where did you go? Family falling out and then sink. Please Lord help them come back. Not grown-up, just want to be big or do they forget how little it seems. Baby crying and mother angry, feed the children and take care of mommy. Stay in school and learn your ABC's and 123 and you can make it. Your parent will be proud of you. Run children run can't deal with it. Society turning wrong instead of right. Help, please the little ones. Future is serious situation.

Romantic Ones

Romantic ones so dreamy
Help you become only human
Take your time and enjoy the little things
They're special and lovable, for we both will never forget them Thanks
for the flowers, the cards and the candy
Thanks for the smiles and laughter
Romantic ones are great memories
Oh best of friends remember

You call to the place and make plans
We start to hold hands
The snow is cold, the fireplace warm
My song is playing, yours is singing
What a wonderful time

Take the steps, let us dance
Come on in, out of the storm, its raining
I see you and you see me, how is the moment we dream
Let us enjoy the day, because soon it will be night ok
We must talk before we go out
One of us loves to hug and hold so tight
We want to be close all night

Think of the time and how romantic it is
Us together, one meaning we and you and me
That's the magical moments to be the romantic ones
All or nothing trying to make it truly something you like

Rethink Notes

Rethink that problem you had or encounter lately
You lost your smile and laughter awhile
Can't find the right way to go

Just think it all empty and not full, going in circles
Keep in mind and most all the time
That you can get a do over never

Never forget we are not perfect people
Was created and changes take time
So always try to go positive and not negative in your situation
Or in life, crisis or circumstances

Try the do over way, keep yourself together
In any weather or storms you may face
Because you will make it through with faith and favor
In your circle and surrounding places anywhere

Prayer and praise are pleasing to hear
Like the spring and summer make it wonderful
In the seasons to come
Enjoy being comfortable and calm
In the areas at hand and beyond
Stay happy and pleasant in all you do and never say never
Just know all things are possible and can be fulfilled
Keep your vision alive

See You Later Never Say Goodbye

Try as you may to see the bright side of things
Did you or I believe in each other or what it lies
You should look at what is pointless and especially what counts
See you later could stay with a person forever
With no might or maybe will you leave or will you stay
Can we be close or move away
Do we have the same interests or are we pretending
Why are emotions high and we can't say goodbye
Now let go to never say goodbye
If you open your mouth to say those words it could be your last
All things that happen
It's the funny things that will not be any more
Will there be dreams and losses
My the distance and separation from one to another
No we can't go back to our views and places are different
Let's say hi and remember to listen
To what I see you and good bye will mean and carry for both
And how it brings new or old circumstances
Maybe happy or sadden

Single Man Moments

A man thinks he is the only one around
Being alone makes him all grown up and a face without a frown
No kids at this time in his life working forget it
Playing video games, having fun and hanging out
The room is dark and bedroom neatness really doesn't matter
Bathing isn't on the list
How many days has he missed
Shaving and grooming aren't his style
No cleaning or laundry at all everything is dirty and messy
Oh awful he don't care
The man knows that cooking is ok
But wishing it was already done or brought in from somewhere This
man is single and loving it
But hopefully one day a woman will be in his life
So they can marry and stop the one person moments
Of being single and he will be alright
Two instead of one and be devoted to it
Pray for him to get his act together
And believe they can do it
Live for years with someone better
Please help him or he will forget.

Single Parent With Child

You are the person, the one who help to bring into the world a child. No it is not a mistake or a headache.

You were given a gift, blessing
And to make the best of your situation, not get rid of it. (Be Responsible)
No you are not alone.
Sometimes it may look that way, but support is all you need.

So keep the faith and believe God is with you and will see you through.
Never neglect or give up that bundle of joy, the precious child that God created and giving you to take care of.
He or she is part of you, so don't look down or be mean.
Always show love and give them time. Things will work out and both of you will grow and help each other.

You are the single parent and that's your baby boy or girl.
Always try to do what's right and your child will show you respect.
Keep your morals and values attach,
it will prove to follow he or she as an adult.
Good news with grace and belief all will.
Live, love and care for the one that's born this day.
One word -WE- you and baby, with love, counting on you.

Situations Happen

While waiting and looking you show up
Come together sitting and talking and feeling comfortable
Our eyes open and daydreaming started
With a clear head and no mind blowing thoughts
We try to relax as the day went on it seem so long

Keeping your cool and not trying to make a fool of yourself
No reaction to some questions just in complete answers
You look back on all that attention with awards and plaques
They are wonderful but don't think education is not important
Trying to be real smart and all that, where are you headed

Friendships or buddies whatever you prefer
Don't mix it up and become lovers that can come to relationships or something
Hope for things much nicer no sign yet just having fun with one
One day you might be surprise
Or time can turn things into years you and him forever

Listen to the old songs and some of the new ones
It all sounds good and makes you groove
Hold onto that time because you might not get it long
It could be gone
Every situation can be different

Good Job, Veterans
(We Salute All)

Whether one or many, our veterans do come forward to serve and protect (us) each other always. You deserve so much more and not be disappointed for the necessary things in life. All of you make up part of this country. Whatever town, state, or country. Let's give our veterans that handshake, those claps or hugs, and please say, "Thank you so much." Our veterans go back a long way, they tell their stories and travel all over. Honor them and be grateful for them.

So, let's come together and show them love and help them live just a little better. They have families and children too, watching and waiting for their return from duty.

Good job, Veterans and God Bless each one of you and your leaders too.

Salute the veterans.

Always.

Something to Think About That Happened In 98'

The President does he want to tell the truth or lie to people everywhere. Decisions aren't clear at companies aboard. People say it don't snow and what is all the white stuff outside. The children are wishing and dreaming of toys and not many kids sleeping, but pretending to get it all, if its affordable. We work, they play and all the time altogether, we should pray. Money spent, presents wrapped and a big tree decorated in the room with a lot of stuff and unwrap paper and special scents. Santa's coming, but you know Jesus birthday is the most important time or event of the year. Can't nobody help us like Jesus. The old is out and the new is in, can't we all just feel the love with who created us. Rejoice in the room. Days and nights, I listen close to the voice of God speaking to me that's right. That divine love and opening arms when he embraces me. He made us and that took a lot. So remember this, you belong to Jesus and that's a fact. I want you to know that life is special every moment you spend, every hour you live and never choose sin, but repent. Don't do all the wrong things. Try to focus on the right things to come. Count your blessings and move on. Thank Jesus every day. Amen

Stand Up Speak and Stay

Who is trying to speak on this matter? We, all, us or nobody. All need to stand up and state who we are, not what we have become and where we are going. We want to stay in a place is it ours or not belonging to someone else. Stop knocking one to another down and some out. Wishing we could do better. Are things getting worse? In each moment have a vision, reach for the important things in life and put all those worldly things to shame. Spend time go to different places and learn the language so you don't have to blame yourself. If you really care speak it loud, stand up so everyone can see the young and the old. Don't distance yourself from the rest. Stay and see what possible can be for all, not just a few. Check what is going on around the world and everybody involved in the world matters. You are part of it, so let's try to regroup and form to a safe outlet and outlook. Catch it before it's too late and share the moment of your ancestors and people who fought the fights (nonviolent) to give you this time now, before it is over. Speak, decide all should read about it, the history not told. Don't run from it. Embrace and learn, stay and stand up

Sunshine Days

Sunshine and it gets bright on you
Skin tone changes and eyes hurting need sunglasses
Where is the shade you say under the tree or tent we go

Sunshine comes up early in the morning and goes down late in the evening
Giving off heat of the day rays and hot nights coming
But we miss it when the weather changes to winter
All we see is white flakes out the window and limp branches
With icy slippery roads and car will not move

Sunshine and heat are summertime elements
To enjoy and entertain like block parties our backyard barbecues
Get-togethers with family and friends
So don't complain about the sunny weather
Have fun and just go out it just might warm your heart
Enjoy the sunny days to come

Super Bowl - Panic

So many people trying to purchase a ticket to the big game
Wearing their favorite jersey and trying to get a good seat
The two teams are waiting for the moment when they take the field
One coin toss and the first ball kick
Hope it will reach the other team shortly
Here we go, it has started
Who will score first
Everyone is excited for more

The fans are watching weather on TV or listening to radio or at their favorite bar Don't let the score be tie
Everyone will be on edge and saying defense and let's go
Some standing up and others sitting trying to not look at who is winning
Is it there team

The end is near and the team that wins will get a trophy
And be the champion for a whole year
The final field-goal or a touchdown gets the gold
A winner or loser good sportsmanship is the key
Good luck to both teams play hard
That's what you hear from the coaches
Remember next year it will get better with two teams coming to this point again called the Super Bowl
Don't panic, people get ready.

Tell The Story

Read the story about his life (Jesus). Read the red letter in writing, take your time and meditate, find your strength and comfort that's sent. Scriptures are good to read, but parables are not make believe. They really happen for all to hear. Just open your mind and unwind. Plenty to take in and a lot to talk about, tell a stranger and tell a friend how to tell the story about his coming. You have questions, he has answers. You need guidance, he has salvation. Bring it to him and he will supply you with what you need, help you make it. (Bring it to him.) If it be peace, love, joy or a friend, he is always present. Just tell the story or read the story about all the great works he has done. Please tell the story to someone. AMEN

The Bubble-Gum Bandit

It's round like a ball and comes in many colors, soft, but chewy. Is it real or gummy? No one really wants to know, think it taste good, but not for sure. The bandit takes the bubble-gum from many machines or just at the childhood store. We wonder what he does with them, eat some and hold the rest. Maybe in the closet or a safe, we guest. Oh! How they love that pretty gum out of the plastic machine, here it comes. Maybe one or two, just got to have a color one. Can't keep it for a day and not even for a week. The bubblegum bandit likes to peep to see, where the next child keeps that one treat. Watch out or you will weep. He took my bubble gum that belonged to me. He a thief (watch him) and put your bubble gum up because it is sweet.

Thank God For Mom

Thank God for mom
Mom is one of a kind
She keeps all in line

Thank God for mom
Mom knows you well
Even when you misbehave
Try to get out of things without telling lies
She can testify, all that you did as a little child indeed
She will show pictures when you were younger
And now you are much older, you say, oh mom put those away
And you begin smiling that's okay

Thank God for mom
Mom sure can cook great
All she asks is that you bring a big appetite
Mom, the one who carries the weight
And is the center of the family traits, family roots
Always show mom some love, because she's the one that prays
Stays, helps and want things right for you
No matter what comes up, she always has a place for you
In her heart, when others do not, mom's right there to pick you up With
arms opened wide and tells you you'll be alright
Thank God for Mom, not just for one day but everyday is her day Show
love, mom is a very special woman in a lot of ways
That mom, warm, loving and mostly forgiving
Love mom and thanks always

Love Matters

Love can be emotional or meaningful
Or beautiful or in between
Friendship or relationship
make things come together and be wonderful
Family's love is important, friend's love just being there
even if no words are spoken.
Love carries many meanings; that word is powerful,
read and apply to your life God's way

Corinthians 1-13: "Love never fails."

Try it this way and find out: love - you and others.

Love -
L - Let's make it last
O - Only One Life
V - Very much from the heart
E - Everlasting and forever

"Keep it simple and with joy."

The Game of Sports

S - to stay fit
P - playing with confidence
O - over and over again
R - relax after it
T - take your time to learn
S - safe and satisfy, you can make it, keep trying

The most little ball. There it is, the golf ball and the racket is a swinging thing, that take a ball to tennis. A basketball is mighty fun, just don't forget to run. A soccer ball is tough and fast try to pass. A football is surely different to many men as you enter. A lane is what you walk down, but a line is there to stop you, so let that bowling ball go. Lights and flashes, sound and noises that when you play pinball, I got you. The table green, the chalk is white, the stick is long, the ball is colorful insight. A game of pool anyone? The net is high. The score is close. What is this volleyball and referee sent to keep the side apart you see. A paddle is required to play and a net in the middle of the table, so long what a beginning. Ping-pong ball light as a feather. All of them in one, make up the name of most great games. Continue to play your game and be good at it. The game better known as the (S-P-O-R-T) activities.

The Gift To Give
(The Master Way)

My master (Jesus) has lead me this far
Direction to walk in his path
To build a firm foundation
Learning to seek his face in all that I do
Order my steps from day to day
Speak to me so that I will know all that you are trying to tell me
All that you have placed around me
From your greatness and goodness
I know and hope you accept the praise of my heart
You are always helpful and calm all my fears
My life should be reflected with joy and your name gets the glory
Help me to always remember that I am never alone
Your protecting love makes it able to face times when we must suffer
Love and forgiveness with the spirit of Jesus
That I will be able to return love and not evil
Jesus you make us, mold us and use us
We pray thanking you for sheltering us
When familiar surroundings fade strength
My wings of faith
I will accept the need to grow and mature
I must wait for help
For my instructions
If I fail through my own lack of wisdom
Let me rely on your unfaltering love and power
Follow your will with eagerness
The surest path to peace

The Golden Rules of Ages

What happened to the rules?
To do wrong is a hit – (paddle or belt)
To talk back – (it might be your face or no lips to feel)
To play wrong – (stay inside in the house you bet)
To stomp your feet – (you better get over here quick)
To walk out and don't care – (you really make your parents mad, hot)
To stay out – (just make it worse, you will get it)
Whatever happened to the golden rules?
Where does this apply to children of today?
Think before you give the right answer to this question
Think hard and long, because today is different from yesterday
We must pray for our children of today, because they are really some of them confused and lost
Where are the rules that apply to these I don't care kids?

The Good Old Days

As far as I can remember on a cool sunny day
The air seem fresh and sky so blue
The grass was green and the clothes were hanging
On the outside line
And all of the neighbor children were playing around
The parents play card games and the flies were flying
And mosquitoes were biting
The telephone pole was where we count
As we played hide and seek
But everyone was happy and nobody was scared
The good old days were fun with laughter
In the air and not a lot to care
What really did happen to the good old days
Where did they go
We just played and played
I will miss days of fun
All these good old days
They aren't here
So they must be done

The Helpers Count

You know the story who saw footprints in the sand
Who thought they were alone
A friend helps you most of the time
The teacher who teaches all year long
To get their students where they belong
The preacher speaks the word
Where all can hear and bring a crowd
Weather man tries to predict the weather
But it takes a crew to record it all
The sportsman the player will play
With two or more call a team
Weightlifter has a competition to do
But needs support to help him the weights are heavy
(made of steel)
A child wants to say their prayers at night
But it takes an adult to recite with them and make it right
A library is full of books
Let's look at the people who read and think
Those are just a few but there are many more to choose from Never
alone that's for sure not no one
It takes all

The Human Bird Feeder

This man came out into the rain, behind a fence that's really not his home and he didn't complain. He feels lonesome, but not ashamed and with a brown bag in his hand you see. This man spreads breads crumbs everywhere indeed. The birds ate and the joy filled the man's heart and after watching for a while, the old man went back inside with his empty brown bag. He was happy and content as can be. His bird friends that fly so many come to stop by. You see all he wanted is to feed them. Rather it was three, but one thing for sure, he knew the birds were especially free and wanted more.

The Jeweler (one-of-a-kind jewel)

One little shop at the top, not many knew how really close it would be. The case was crystal clear with a neat design. No one has seen around it, when you open it, that jewel was breathtaking. The glow was so radiant that the owner said, "How long will you be staring at it?" Face lit up, this stone cost plenty and is a keepsake. Not to be pawned off, but cared for by someone special and can't be traded. One piece to remember the jewel, when back in the lock box and waiting to see who will buy it to enjoy and appreciate now and forever, a lifetime. Piece, oh beautiful it was to see, someday it might be for me.

The Leading Role

It's not easy to be the star quarterback of the team
The president got his handful of all the people in the White House
And the communities and neighborhoods, cities and the streets
This is not an easy task, someone higher must
You can't be left alone
You can start but hold on
The job can make you hard
Everyone can stride to be the leading star
Keep in mind what it takes to bring about change and achievements
That you adapt, tap into all your good senses to move
On to acquire all those things people said you could accomplish
You are having a leading role so let's acknowledge it
For now and always remember the one who helps
To give you that start, carry him in your heart
Rather it be you or me playing this role
Make very sure that there are no holes to get you in deeper
When you only want to excel to the next place to care for people

The Light Is Bright

You have a light you see
But it is not clear as it can be
You must let it shine and keep it bright and beautiful
DIVINE
By praying and keeping it holy within
I love this light you see
No one can take if away from me
IT IS FREE
So keep it in mind
This light you have, God gave it to me
So I am going to let it shine and glow all the time

The Missing Love Letter

It fell under the table. I opened it and the words came with a rush. I could only think of all the times we said so many words and couldn't say them in person. You wrote, just what my heart was feeling. It skipped a beat as I continued to read it and all the love you poured out just brought me to tears. The letter was the best one yet. Should I call you or just let it be, but my thoughts were with you and the moments we shared. Holding the letter in my hand, I had to really sit down and take it all in. The letter I didn't get in time. Too much to bare, this missing love letter that changed so many things in our friendship and relationship could have made a total difference for us as one. What to do or say? Both wonder if it could have been me. I could have been the lady of your life. Not just the letter not found until now. (A-M-L-L) found later (wow)

The Morning Feeding (The Word)

My friend (Jesus), wakes me up early in the morning and as my eyes are open, I begin to realize it is time to be fed (The Word). I open the Holy book and begin to read and be filled from the beginning and the end. This feeding is free and always forever. I don't have to pay no one, or stop getting this feeding my friend take good care of me. I always thank my friend, because I know that I am full for that day and the joy is all over me. My friend is always lifting me up to get this wonderful feeding, (The Word) and to keep me going. My friend sees that I am prepared, so I love and care about my friend by a thanks and prayer. Jesus is the answer for anything the world offer. Thank you Jesus. Every feeding you will want more and more. The Word, the beginning and the end!

*"The Lord is good and his love endures forever,
His faithfulness continues through all generations."*

- Psalm 100:51

The People's Man (MJ)

M-Magical as he could be in his era
I-In his own way
C-Crowds adore his moves
H-Hand in a glove
E-Ever with us
A-All care about his family
L-Loved by his children
J-Joy of dancing and singing
A-Actions unstoppable
C-Created in all forms dancing
K-Kind and gentle, not many words spoken
S-Singing and surprising with his talent
O-On the stage going different places, putting small smiles on faces and some crying
N-No one song is enough, his music still lives on in all generations young and old

Remember Michael Jackson, a young icon gone. But the media, some people and other folks didn't make it simple, but he could really perform. From wearing an afro to a different style and a hat and he made the money and made entertainment bigger than ever. That's MJ - moonwalk dancer

The Reflection Of A Bird

A bird was tapping on the window outside and I wonder why he would go from corner to corner tapping away. I just sit and watch this bird as it would tap away. Oh, the bird was not very smart. It's reflection was looking him back into the window. I guess he will never get tired, because it really couldn't win. I've never seen a bird so determined trying to tap his way inside from the outside of the window. He thought he seen another bird, but the bird was really the same bird tapping away and trying to prove a point of the reflection of a bird on the window who came to tap. I will let the bird be.

The Secret Place

As you walk in, try to remember
Come let's go to the best place ever
It is quiet where you can collect your thoughts
And your mind corrects as one
Communication is essential and very real
I will wait for you and help you through all your storms Disappointments, worries and give the best comfort of all
The one, Lord you will meet and greet at this secret place
You can rejoice and call upon the Lord now and forever
I'll wait for you, my child to come and be used
For an awesome unique way from this day
Come forward and live
Amen

The Trumpet Sounds

Oh what a great instrument to sound
It's tune is so different and likable to hear
It would give you the command and announce
Let us sing, shout out and get ready
For an experience never seen

This day will come and all will hear the trumpet sound very clear There
will be many, but only takes one to know the different
And what it will bring

Rejoice, peace, hope and willingness to be at the great gathering For the
King of Kings and the Lord of Lord will arrive
Are you ready, let's all give thanks and praise to our Lord
Jesus has come to take us home to the kingdom
What a glorious time we will have
No more of this and no more that

Many will wonder and all will hear his voice
Let the trumpet sound and let it be loud and heard
Let's get it together before the great celebration begins
Holy, Holy, Holy almighty king you are worthy to be praised
Glory to your name Jesus, our king
Let the trumpet sound
Our celebration will be awesome to our king

The World Is So Big

Why is the world so big? It's made up of people, places, and things which God makes everything. The world is round shaped and always rotating from country to country, city the city and state to state. Each part of the world is different and unique. You can go everywhere to greet, travel by plane, buses and boats, but most of all by trains at night. Lots of people, many kids and small children growing, babysitting by nanny keepers and family, teaching each other, having traditional meetings and dinners. The weather, the sun, the moon and rain from the sky, feeling hot, warm, cool and cold. Grass, plants, flowers and trees make up the part of this big world you see, but most of all variety food, snacks, beverages and sweets. Make up your daily eating habits, treats, books, papers, money, pictures make up the rest of the world literature and spending in the big world. That's spinning and that's plenty.

There Is Hope

There is hope you know
In all that you say and do
Just keep your head up
And time will heal all things it seems

Never feel discourage or dismay
Always remember God cares the most
That's why he made us
Family and friends come together when it is long overdue
Or of sorrow in some cases you see

Remember to pray always
And try to hold on to faith
God is trying to get through to you
Give your attention to him
And you will get real love from Heaven
That's what God sends

Take the time to care and love each other
That's not much to ask
Your heart should send a true meaning and not a lie
God wants this from each and every one of us
Repent and watch

For time is more important than ever before
Hope is a big part of it all
Just have H-O-P-E

Turn it in to Faith (Heb. 11-1)

This Was You My Child

You weighed a healthy size, got five fingers each and toes. Your smile was like sunlight, hair is so full and eyes that had an awesome look. You grew and grew, got taller. Your first bottle was gone, milk from a cup was new, took some time to get use too. Your clothes were neat. Matching was easy and shoes just right. Your birthday came fast. Cake and ice cream was a blast. Thanksgiving spent with family and giving thanks. Christmas was quiet. You opened every presents you got. Paper unwrapping was your style. Giving you money was a surprise. Most of the cards you would sit aside. The first phone that you got was placed under your bed. The sound it made, you couldn't wait to answer it and then smile and say, "What's my number?" Your mother and grandmother who care to see you get on your way from pre-k, elementary, high school and even to the military. We were with you and so happy. Both of us just loved and cared about a baby, a child and a teenager, then a man. My, how time does fly. Keep your heart close and your mind sharp, knowledge and wisdom are good to have. Always be willing to learn. One day you will be a better man than he. You will see! You can do it, try and never give up. A big world and a lot of opportunities for success. Dream big, keep your head up and wonderful things can happen at once. You are a winner and my son.

Those Sleepless Places

Rather a cardboard box and a sack of items. An old cot or worn-out mattress, not a room. Under the bridge or an open park bench, they wonder is it going to be a restless night. Do you help to get them a better place? The weather seems colder and not as warm with little covering or blankets to protect their bodies. No words spoken. Maybe a sign that says lunch, a job or a few cents. Just a safe place of some sort. Morning will come, the days long. Where will you go? Trying to find another area or spot. Feelings of shock. It seems to be sleepless places. Some odd and others trashy and smelly. Hope for something better. Pray for those with less out in the open world and struggling stressful, but not complaining to any. Making the best of some things, with no money. Let us help all who can give. If you got, show love for many or anyone coming or going out there who are needy.

To Be Closer To You

Who are you? Who am I?
We are two people from separate sides
The person with no words, no feeling, not even a friendly hi
What would I give to say hello ... I ask do you really want to know
We'd both find ourselves in a world of confusion
A face not even smiling turning to sadness
To communicate is to mumble, to cry not even a tear
To read is to find the words   To write is to take a lot of thinking
So I just come to one line to remember try to be friendly
Oh why, oh how can I be the person you talk to this moment.

Three Little Elderly Women

The elderly women walk alone with their canes and glasses on
Traveling to see and visiting at the time
Saying to the person which way do we go
We really don't know
Please help us to find our way
This place is so big and tall we are so small
We are telling you to take us to the mall
With canes in hand and moving right along
They decided it was time to go watch out
For the three elderly women that dress similar
But is nice as can be trying to get from point A to B
Walking at just the right speed to make it to their vehicle
The three were talking and smiling
As they arrived to their destination and then said to all bye-bye
And take care until their next visit
The three

Time

Day by day a little at a time
To keep your thoughts and your mind
I'd like to see the spring break through
The flowers are beautiful and a lovely scene to me
You got to go different places and do different things
But time is not your important gain
With day or night you think it comes and go and it will be alright
But I tell you time is passing on and you shouldn't be wasting it alone
Rather you are young or old never go back
Because time is surely not staying still
Move, you can start early or you can stay later
But time move on and as an eye winks
Look at your watch take notice of the clock
Check out the movement of time a solid fact
It will never stand still or stop
Just remember that time come like session and then disappear
Can you recall your events dates and laughter of time
What has time meant to you
Most say they got time but it doesn't stay there very long
And before you know it is completely gone
Taking away, vanish disappear can't recall
But it is simple time waits for no one
Not you not me not even little babies no one
What have you done with your time every day
Have you used it in the right way
Time to live
Time to watch
Time to sing
Time to be
But most of your time should be spent with me (God)

To Discover Oneself (Your Vision)

Let yourself go there
To a place of wonderful things
The place that has everything
All is good nature
All the right moods
And no sadness
The place of discovery can be with you
Can you help yourself to get there
Or are you tied up in old and past memories
Try the new and forget the old
Keep in mind that you're wasting precious time
Discover the new and different places to see
And more things to do in reality
Better known as your vision of oneself

To Give and Accept Love

The child who missed his doggie
Aging parents who told and show love before passing
The rescue dog that just wants a home and was a big help to the blind.
The mailman that delivers the mail so cheerful every morning and says how are you doing?

Preacher tries to teach and help others to receive love and stop all the hate. The nurse or doctor make a visit to each room to say it will get better.
Your neighbor waves his or her hand across the way just to say have a good day.

Bus driver takes the kids to school. It is just around the bend.
Keep a smile for your teacher that you meet, because it is the first day of a new year.

We all got to give (accept love.) It is beautiful and wonderful in so many forms and not to harm any of us, but remember this love is the greatest word in this world of ours.

To My Son Special One

There is a special person that I know who makes me laugh and smile awhile. He is. Wonderful, delightful and precious and smart to me. Dear God thank you for my son. I hope you get the best in life. To this special person, I say keep your head up high and always reach for the sky. Rather your objective is big or small, remember that all these things will be there. Nicest, kindest respect and good manners will be with you along the way. To grow in learning, sharing and caring. Reading can help you too. Self-esteem and your confidence remain. I love you my son always. To you I say, if I have helped you in anyway, I am proud and happy as can be. When you came into the world, I knew you were special to me. So whole that dear to your heart and like a face in a picture window, our love will never part. So to you my special person and friend, you are the best son, all in one. You are one of a kind, so keep the faith and prayers in mine. Keep your hand in God's hands. You should always want to be yourself and not a follower, but a leader to your own destiny or become your own person and friend. I love you my son and you will someday be a man. Make mommy proud of you. You will make it, I know you can. My son is very important and special to me. Son always remember how we helped you to grow and taught you to learn and let God do the rest. Ok, I love you.

Twice A Rainbow

Have you ever seen it twice with wonderful colors and it looked really nice it always came after the rain, an arch from one end to the other? It is so amazing you can't stop looking at it. You can walk, drive or ride and see the beauty in the sky, wondering how long it will be there, for a couple of minutes or a few. When God created the rainbow it was an awesome sign and a promise that last a lifetime. Keep that beauty in mind and never think that it isn't real, because it is and always appears in a different area, a field or path, a pasture or in the original. If you see it twice, that makes it really nice and good things can happen. Believe in miracles and rainbow sightings. They could be everywhere. Not in one or two places, here and beyond. A rainbow it's so divine in nature, you must look more than once to really take it all in. Colorful and beautiful scene.

Two Men Walk

Two men were walking down the walk, both were in conversation intense. One man to another man, as they reach their separate walks, they embrace each other and were on their way. I wonder who is the sinner and the saint? God only knows the truth, but as their journey ended with no turning back to see, when each person was out of sight, the door opened and they went their ways. Will these two men walk together again or just think about the moment, about a walk with different beginning. The end may be sensible you see, but both would like to know what will happen to them. A walk for nothing. A walk for something. What will it be? Their ending.

Unity For All

Rather a group society or charity
We all need fellowship with the Almighty
Strengthen us in our work
Teach us to love, have mercy and pardon our wrongs
Forgiving our shortcomings and courage to undertake the battle
Keep us close to you oh lord
And always seek your face open our eyes that we will see
All the beauty green and peaceful waters flow
Supply our needs with an overflow
And see your children have a home
Give us wisdom and understanding
Clothe us for the cold and virtuous
Teach us not to judge but to always show love
Standby us through all circumstances
Sense our blessing and living in joy
Let everyone be saved in your name Jesus
Name above all names
Guide us, lead us and protect and let's all shout hallelujah
God be with us all unity
God give us the right mind heart and soul
Because we know you are in control always

Unwanted Person

To never tell a story
To always see things negatively
You can't imagine what you are missing
Can't think of the future
I never feel strong and wise
Just wasting time and talking jive
Nobody caring so that's what this message describes
The feeling of unwanted and let down
Hopes and desires to feel a surface of emptiness and alone
Not a friend to call on
Just confusion and pain
Can't really explain
Just not friendly
Just unwanted
Just feel shame
Can't throw the blame

Wait on Your Dream or Miracles

Why rush time away
Making things happen faster than supposed to be (original)
We try so hard to wish for a day to go by
And hope all goes our way
But think for a moment and decide
If you could fly or jump to the sky
Touch the moon or run the distance to a city unknown
Picture yourself making buildings or creating your own planet
We ask ourselves could this really happen
For we wait on a miracle
Or dream a motion a thought or want to do just that
Keep looking and wishing for all to be real
And maybe just maybe it will
It's your miracle so watch and see what comes out
Could be both who knows what will happen
And when it's possible
Dream and Miracles

We Need Conquerors

People prevail over it to overcome and make it
Never give in or step out of place
But stand up, claim what is really yours
Gain success and overcome the obstacles that keep us stressed
Don't be overwhelmed
Hold your head up and think win
I am a winner, not a sinner trying to make it in
Don't make a mistake, God love promises are sent
Protection can work your way
Be a good servant for a life sake
That's your right, establish yourself, follow his example
Then giving God the glory
We are conquers
They are needed, so let's shout
Yes we are and mean it

What Can I Do? Oh Lord

What can I do to make it simple and plain? Jesus loves you this I know. His Word is true and eternal too.

Keep it close and never doubt. Jesus knows what we are all about. What can I do to make you see? It is written and it is told. What more can I do oh Lord?

I want a relationship with you and maybe just maybe it will help someone else too. Oh lord, what can I do? Let me be free. Let me fellowship, but most of all let me be able to pray.

Oh, Lord help me to be all that you want me to be. What can I do truly for thee? Speak to me O' Lord. Teach me how. Let me move forward and you always keep an eye to see how I'm doing and what I have done. I will always remember asking what can I do O' Lord to be a servant and hearing those words, well done.

What Does It Mean?

To start with baby steps is (the beginning)
To fall it every time (you get up) means a lot
The words hold on and everything will be alright
They say I can't and I will not turn so let's try and yes you can do right
I want to believe and dream the dream
Keep your vision in your site and one day it will work out
Never say that it looks bad
Just remember God is good and able to help at any minute or hour
What does it mean to keep on being strong when you are feeling weak
Praying for all and not just one or their faults
Reading the words and asking for forgiveness
and showing love accordingly
Take a second and reflect on all that you have been giving and been
blessed beyond your days in each year's coming and going
This means more than being empty and not caring about nothing
What does it mean?

What Makes One Cry

One cry today for some odd reason
One didn't feel good about being around people
One heart was sad, eyes burning
One ask God for forgiveness
One not perfect you see
One got a lot going on in me
One try to do right most of the time
Because sometimes one get out of line
One cries sometimes, feels blue and wants to become brand new
If one could just stop the tears that flow down your cheeks
What makes one unhappy
One want to know why they crying
Sometimes feels good but hurts inside
One guess it is like medicine of some sort
You shake it and take it and hope to feel better
One will try to stop crying and maybe just maybe
I'll feel a whole lot cheery with laughter

When Are You Going To Learn

That money don't grow on trees and stop asking mom please. Go to work and make an effort. Good things could really look up and happen. You heard of the birds and bees, but that only means baby bottles and even pampers or diapers. You choose going out every night, shaking your booty and living it up. What about school or college? That's real not playing, but planning staying away or skipping your classes. Education is important. Why you go around lying and cussing? Those cigarettes is going to take you out. Even taking things that don't belong to you will only get you in a place that's crowded and evil. You might have to fight to stay on track or be taken out, by others you don't like and keep watching your back. Parent or guardian might have raised you, but think about the person you want to become learn and grow to be someone great. Be you! Only learn to appreciate. That's a start!

With Open Eyes

I woke up this morning and I know why
It was you dear Lord waiting to hear my morning prayer
I lift my eyes to the sky and this is what came out of my cry
Thank you Lord for everything
Thank you Lord for another day
Help me through the good and the bad
I will always learn to pray
You can guide me and help me to be your child in eternity
Thank you Lord
I will always try to open my eyes for heaven bound glory ride

When Man Says No God Says Yes

You said you were going to help me and you didn't, man says no I will
help you and take care of you
God says yes, come to me
Needs to be met, yard work piling up, house cleaning
Lacking man says no, but God says yes
I will send you a help mate
Money low, job not sure, food on the table, bills higher
Man says no, God says yes don't worry it's all covered
I will make a way, yes it's done
Children all grown, can't wait to be gone
No laughter, lonely, sadness, man says no
God says yes, you are not alone, I'm with you
Always now and forever, until the end
People busy, traffic moving, laws changing
Kids disobeying, elders are disrespected, what is going on
Man says no, God says yes, train them up in the way of the Lord
And I will guide them, lead them and show them the way to go Man No,
God is Yes
Always

When The Two Do Not Match

Take these things for example
One shoe was blue and the other red
The boat you thought was a ship
The car you drive you said it could fly only.... a car
Your house was huge, but you didn't get it
There's others living in huts
Your cash was low, then you had a plastic card, plenty of interest Books
were hot, but the internet was tops
The t.v. doesn't work
So you all want to go to the theater that night
Food smells good, but the fruit was no good
Child didn't listen, you shouted I am going to get you
Popcorn was popping
Who's doing all that rapping, is it you
As you can see all these things not matching
Makes for good or better to come and face reality
Let's see turn into a look and other things and people are hooked On the
things of today, that's a fact not an act
Not the beginning, but a crazy ending
No Match

Win or Lose

To win means everything is great
Your day was good
You feel excellent
You jump for joy
You will really enjoy it
And that is alright
To lose means you're down
Your day was a disaster
Your mood is it so upbeat
No talking
No smiling
Just a plain old frown
To win means three great words
You got it
To lose means two awful words
Not now
But both words rely on you
The person and how they want to feel like for that day
If that is win or lose.

Write On Paper

Can you remember the right way to put or write your name on paper? Then come your words and numbers and don't forget those letters, alphabets on paper. Take a minute and look at how it adds up and today is so different. Computers, laptop, iPad, internet and many other gadgets. Not using your mind, easily as can be. Thinking is not your greatest thing these days and in time. You see, check out the little kids running around talking, rapping and singing. Wo, oh baby, and me take the time that you use. Put it in good use and not loose. What are you looking to do to help? The little kids survive this. Make a pledge to support the kids. They are the future and not gangs, but need protection. Each other's got to stop fighting and bullying and grow up to be somebody special. Nobody wants to get involved, but the kids are going to the wrong side. Let's pray tonight that all the kids be alright with love, peace and hope. We will believe they say, I can be a teacher or doctor or president and these are great roles. If you stick it out and live to see it in this world for kids sake.

You Are Not Excused (because of circumstances)

You don't say anything awful or upsetting to your parents or teachers, cussing and swearing to women and ladies. Why do you go out and think it is right to steal and to rob taking things that aren't your own? Knocking people around a carrying dangerous weapons. Trying to be tough and rough for others, telling people to give up their hard earned money. Wearing your pants down and acting like clowns, caught up in the rap wearing colors so you standout. Some can't count to nine, but you throw up your fingers with signs. You said your father wasn't in your life, but when do you come in and be the man not only for yourself, but for your children and extended families. Do you care about your siblings or is it all about the streets(that's negative)? You weren't born this way. You grow up and changed to be a follower of some sort, not a role model, a leader of positive things you could accomplish right. What happened along the way? A mother, father, brother or somebody told you what can happen out there. You choose the path or the play. What role is going to carry you far in this life or out of the world? Go with your decision made early and not later with no excuse. Just try to succeed, it makes a difference with faith and believing in you. (Choose your ways for the better.)

You Can Make It With God's Help

What can I say? Oh, Lord what can I do, but pray hoping he makes it day by day. He shuffles his paper and use little stud pencils. Oh, what can I do? You can make it. Tests and quizzes, programs and reading. Oh, Lord what can I do?

After school trips and baseball cleats, hot dogs and soda, french fries and pizza. Oh, what a treat!

Getting up mornings and business as usual, breakfast and bath. Clothes and shoes, books in his pack and not missing a day, he is sent. Oh, Lord he can make it.

He's getting taller and I'm looking shorter. Working on a computer and playing his trumpet. Oh, how surprising, but you can make it, with God's help.

Look to the future and moving out of the past. Oh, Lord help him know just ask, keep on praying, keep on praising. You can make it. For God says so and he knows all.

You Don't Miss Me

Did you call me when you were hurting
And say you don't care or can't get a message through
You try to write but no paper or pen in your sight
While you are looking for things in the dark
I look at your picture and see a face not smiling
But you are turning wrinkles
No words or laughter just you telling your boys
That you are happy but that's not true
You got the blues sadly, why did it happen
Your pride and you took the ride
Thought it was awesome, but look at the mess that was made
You in one place and I in another is crazy
Is that my friend or a stranger, can't tell at this moment
Don't miss me for the miserable times, but remember me
For all the wonderful times and thoughtful words
And our favorite songs, then you can miss me
Ok Mr. The Man, the friend or just a stranger
You don't miss me, apart can be good
But always take a look at what we had and could be
Growing, you and me together, time spent and time gone by
What did you really hope for?

You say Peace they say Piece

This world seems so twisted now
Handle it likely and not really caring
People talk peace holding signs saying keep calm
Wearing colors or faces of another
Embracing each other hands up high freely
Claiming no harm others get pieces
To use it wrongly and never think twice
To places and proceed to use it like it's nothing is dangerous
No matter what kind innocent humans being harmed
A baby, child or teen or parent stop all this madness
Think about the next time you bring out the choice peace or piece
Will it help or hurt a family, community, group or town or a nation
What peace/piece will you bring forward
Let all decide, will you make a difference or cause problems
Think about this before instructing in any direction
You will go with it sorrow, pain or something ugly
Or stay calm, steadfast and diffuse the situation
Or why you need to do something positive or go negative
And do nothing and proceed to the complaints from any
And act crazy or come out peacefully

Your Care Means A Lot

A mother comforts her child
The teacher learns the student
The preacher speaks the word
The choir sings the songs
A father isn't supposed to provoke his children
Men and women need encouragement
Everyone should love the other
Be a grateful servant and always respect your elders
Always help the poor and care for the sick
Treat your neighbor with good manner
Stay firm and ask for guidance and protection
Be still and listen to and know that I care about you
And you to all acknowledge the truth
Remember me my child one of you said
Who is this they really care about me
Glorify God, thank you and help me daily and stay by my side
Love is so great and means a lot
You care

Note From The Author

Thank God for my gift and talent, first always. I am a person who loves to write, read, and enjoy music. My work is original so I hope everyone enjoyed it. I am blessed to be able to write about so many different topics. I am humble and sincere to all I can help by writing this book. I have waited so long to fulfill this goal of mine and now is the time. Never give up on your goals or dreams. I hope this book doesn't make anyone uncomfortable; if so, I am deeply sorry. This is my opinion only.

- Lenore Miles

www.ingramcontent.com/pod-product-compliance
Lightning Source LLC
Chambersburg PA
CBHW020910090426
42736CB00008B/565